PLANT LEAVES

David M. Schwartz *is an award-winning author of children's books, on a wide variety of topics, loved by children around the world.* Dwight Kuhn's *scientific expertise and artful eye work together with the camera to capture the awesome wonder of the natural world.*

For a free color catalog describing Gareth Stevens Publishing's list of high-quality books and multimedia programs, call 1-800-542-2595 (USA) or 1-800-461-9120 (Canada). Gareth Stevens Publishing's Fax: (414) 225-0377.

Library of Congress Cataloging-in-Publication Data

Schwartz, David M.
    Plant leaves / by David M. Schwartz; photographs by Dwight Kuhn.
        p. cm. — (Look once, look again)
    Includes bibliographical references (p. 23) and index.
    Summary: Introduces, in simple text and photographs, the leaves of moss,
cabbage, ferns, sundew, maple, and the colored leaves of autumn.
        ISBN 0-8368-2428-8 (lib. bdg.)
    1. Leaves—Juvenile literature. [1. Leaves.] I. Kuhn, Dwight, ill. II. Title.
III. Series: Schwartz, David M. Look once, look again.
QK649.S36   1999
575.5'7—dc21   99-18608

This North American edition first published in 1999 by
Gareth Stevens Publishing
1555 North RiverCenter Drive, Suite 201
Milwaukee, Wisconsin 53212 USA

First published in the United States in 1998 by Creative Teaching Press, Inc., P.O. Box 6017, Cypress, California, 90630-0017.

Text © 1998 by David M. Schwartz; photographs © 1998 by Dwight Kuhn. Additional end matter © 1999 by Gareth Stevens, Inc.

Printed in the United States of America

1 2 3 4 5 6 7 8 9 03 02 01 00 99

PLANT LEAVES

by David M. Schwartz

photographs by Dwight Kuhn

A SPRINGBOARDS INTO SCIENCE SERIES

Gareth Stevens Publishing

MILWAUKEE

These leaves make a thick, spongy carpet
that feels good under your feet.

This type of moss grows on logs, stumps, rocks, and soil. It looks like a soft, green mat, and it feels like one, too. If you look closely, you will see that the mat is made of many separate plants. Each plant has its own stem and leaves.

When these colors appear, a leaf will soon …

...fall. Why? A leaf falls when it gets no sap from the tree. In autumn, sap tubes begin to close. Sap cannot enter the leaf. The leaf dies and falls to the ground.

People eat leaves like these in coleslaw and sauerkraut.

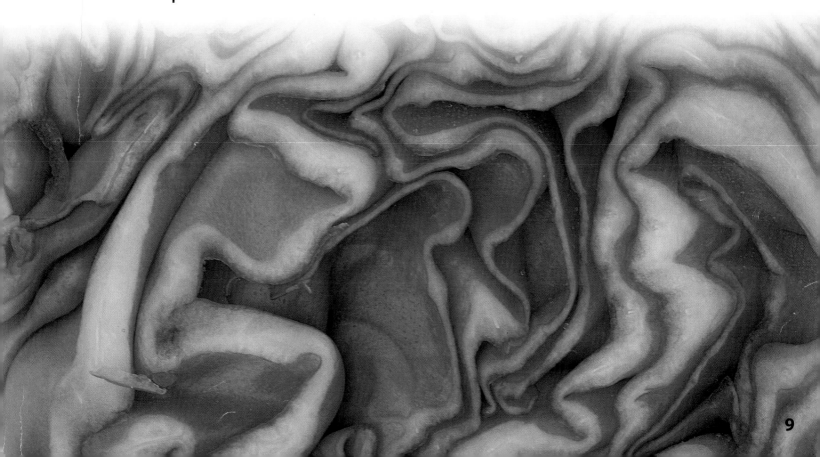

A head of cabbage is made of leaves. The leaves grow on a short, thick stalk. They wrap around the stalk to make a ball. Some cabbage leaves are green, and some are red. When a cabbage head is cut through, the curly leaves make a beautiful pattern.

10

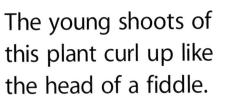

The young shoots of this plant curl up like the head of a fiddle.

When ferns come up in spring,
their shoots are called fiddleheads.
The fiddleheads uncurl into frilly,
pointy leaves called fronds.
Fern fronds can carpet
a forest's floor.

These curvy lines are made by an insect. The insect tunnels through a leaf like a miner tunneling through the Earth.

An insect lays its eggs inside a leaf. When an egg hatches, a larva comes out. It is called a leaf miner.
It eats its way through the leaf, making a tunnel as it goes. When the larva becomes an adult, it flies away to find a mate. Females lay their eggs inside another leaf.

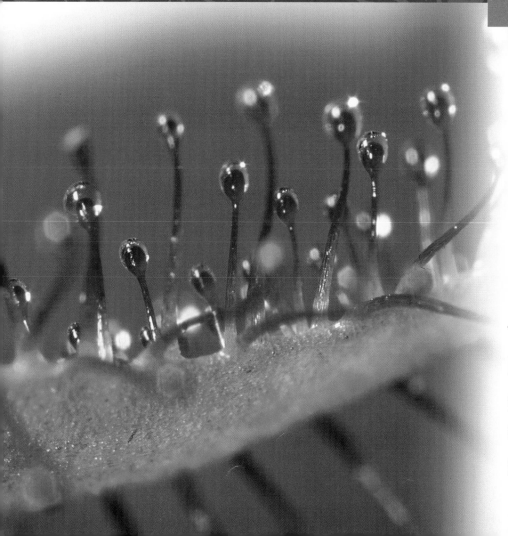

These are not drops of dew, but they are a pretty sight glistening in the sun. If you are a fly, you don't want to get too close!

15

The leaves of the sundew plant
are covered with long tentacles.
A drop of sticky gum sits
at the tip of each tentacle.
When a fly lands on a sundew,
it sticks to the gum.
The plant oozes more gum,
and the fly cannot get free.
Slowly, the sundew
digests the fly.

It is spring. These young leaves have just appeared. Where were they during winter? They were packed inside a bud.

All winter, the maple tree has no leaves, but it has many buds. Buds are little cases that protect the tiny leaves inside. In spring, sap flows through the trees. The buds swell. The leaves inside grow larger and larger. One day, the buds burst open. Then, the tree has leaves.

A.

B.

C.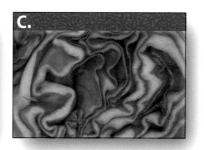

D.

E.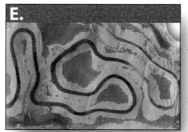

F.

G.

Look closely. What do you see?

A. Moss

B. Autumn leaves

C. Cabbage

D. Ferns

E. Leaf miner

F. Sundew

G. Maple

How many were you able to identify correctly?

bud: a small swelling on a branch or stem that contains a leaf or flower before it develops and opens.

dew: moisture that collects on cool surfaces, such as grass, usually during the night.

digest *(v)***:** to break food down into a form that can be used by the body.

fern: a type of green plant that usually has feathery leaves called fronds.

fiddlehead: a young fern.

frond: the leaf of a fern or a palm tree.

larva: the wingless stage of an insect's life, after it has hatched from an egg and before it becomes an adult. A caterpillar is one kind of larva.

moss: a small, green plant that grows on damp ground, tree trunks, or rocks.

oozes: flows out slowly.

protect: to keep something safe.

sap: the liquid that flows inside a plant, carrying food to different parts of the plant.

shoot *(n)***:** the tender part of a plant that has just begun to grow.

stalk *(n)***:** the part of a plant that supports a leaf or flower.

swell: to get larger because of pressure from the inside.

tentacle: the narrow, flexible part of a plant or animal that is used for grasping and moving.

ACTIVITIES

Eating Leaves
People around the world eat the leaves of many different kinds of plants. Visit the produce section of a local supermarket and make a list of leaves that people eat. Put a check mark by the leaves you have eaten.

Insects, Beware!
The sundew is one kind of carnivorous plant — a plant that captures insects for food. Learn about other types of carnivorous plants, such as the pitcher plant and Venus fly trap, from a book or the Internet. How do each of these plants capture and digest insects?

Leave It to Me
Make a list of animals that depend on leaves for food, to build their nests, or to prepare their homes. In what other ways do they use leaves?

Make a Terrarium
Make a terrarium by putting a layer of gravel in the bottom of a fishbowl or small tank. Add several inches (centimeters) of potting soil. Gently pat the soil to keep it in place. Plant some moss, ferns, and small green plants in the bowl. Cover the terrarium with plastic wrap, leaving a small opening on one edge. Place the terrarium in a sunny location, and add water as needed to keep the soil damp.

Leaf Collection
With an adult's help, collect a variety of leaves of different sizes and shapes. Press the leaves between pieces of paper towel inside a large book. After a few days when the leaves are dry and flat, arrange them on construction paper, and glue them in place. Label each leaf by name and where you found it.

More Books to Read

Bloodthirsty Plants (series). Victor Gentle (Gareth Stevens)

Ferns. Theresa Greenaway (Steck-Vaughn Library)

A First Look at Leaves. Millicent Selsam (Walker)

It Could Still Be a Leaf. Allan Fowler (Childrens Press)

Mighty Tree. Dick Gackenbach (Harcourt Brace Jovanovich)

The Nature and Science of Leaves. Exploring the Science of Nature (series).
  Jane Burton and Kim Taylor (Gareth Stevens)

Videos

Carnivorous Plants. (Pyramid Media)

Ferns. (Films for the Humanities & Sciences)

How Plants Get Food. (MBG Videos)

Web Sites

www.mobot.org/MBGnet/sets/temp/leaves/index.htm

www.muohio.edu/dragonfly/tree.htm/x

Some web sites stay current longer than others. For further web sites, use your search engines to locate the following topics: *ferns, leaves, maples, mosses, oaks, photosynthesis, sundews,* and *trees.*

INDEX